WHERE IS MY
TOWN?

by Robin Nelson

first step nonfiction

Lerner Publications Company · Minneapolis

I live in a **town.**

A town is a group of
neighborhoods.

I live in my town with my family.

I go to school in my town.

I shop in my town.

I play in my town.

My town is in my state.

There are towns
all over the world.

Some towns have a lot of people but very little land.

These towns are called
cities.

Some towns have more land
and fewer people.

These towns are called **suburbs.**

Some towns have a lot of
land and not a lot of people.

These towns are in the
country.

Where is my town?

My town is in my state,
where I live with my family.

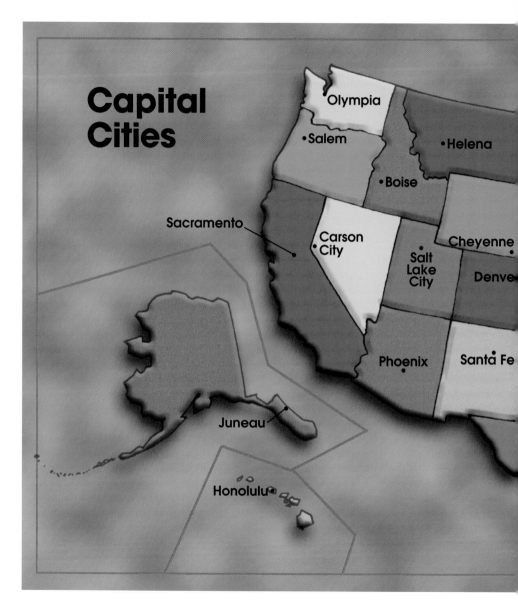

Capital Cities

Olympia

•Salem

•Helena

•Boise

Sacramento

Carson
•City

Cheyenne
•

Salt
Lake
City

Denve

Phoenix

Santa Fe

Juneau

Honolulu

Bismarck

Saint
Paul

Pierre

Madison

Lansing

Montpelier

Augusta

Concord

Boston

Albany

Providence

Hartford

Des
Moines

Lincoln

Topeka

Springfield

Columbus

Indianapolis

Harrisburg

Trenton

Dover

Annapolis

Washington, D.C.

Charleston

Jefferson
City

Frankfort

Richmond

Oklahoma
City

Nashville

Raleigh

Little
Rock

Atlanta

Columbia

Jackson

Austin

Montgomery

Tallahassee

Baton
Rouge

Town Facts

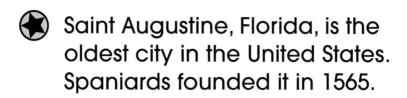 Saint Augustine, Florida, is the oldest city in the United States. Spaniards founded it in 1565.

★ Jamestown, Virginia, was the first permanent British settlement in North America. About 100 colonists established it in 1607.

★ The city with the largest population in the world is Tokyo, Japan.

★ The U.S. city with the most people is New York City.

The most common town names in the United States are:
1. Fairview
2. Midway
3. Oak Grove
4. Franklin
5. Riverside
6. Centerville
7. Mount Pleasant
8. Georgetown
9. Salem
10. Greenwood

Glossary

 cities – places where many people live and work. A city is a large town.

 country – an area away from a city where few people live

 neighborhoods – homes and people who live around you

 suburbs – areas on or close to the outer edge of a city

 town – a place where people live and work. A town is smaller than a city.

Index

The photographs in this book are reproduced through the courtesy of: © Corbis Royalty Free, front cover, p. 16; © D. Yeske/Visuals Unlimited, pp. 2, 22 (bottom); © Patrick Cone, pp. 3, 12, 22 (middle); © Trip/H. Rogers, p. 4; © Tom Edwards/Visuals Unlimited, p. 5; © David Young-Wolff/Stone, p. 6; © Mark Gibson/Visuals Unlimited, p. 7; © Joseph Sohm/Corbis, p. 8; © Wolfgang Kaehler, pp. 9, 11, 13, 14, 22 (top, second from top, second from bottom); © M. Bryan Ginsberg, p. 10; © John Green/Visuals Unlimited, p. 15; © Gerard Fritz/Photo Agora, p. 17.

Lerner Publications Company
A division of Lerner Publishing Group
241 First Avenue North
Minneapolis, MN 55401 U.S.A.

Website address: www.lernerbooks.com

Library of Congress Cataloging-in-Publication Data

Nelson, Robin, 1971–
    Where is my town? / by Robin Nelson.
        p.   cm. — (First step nonfiction)
    Includes index.
    ISBN: 0–8225–0190–2 (lib. bdg. : alk. paper)
    1. Cities and towns—Juvenile literature. 2. City and town life—Juvenile literature.
    3. Family life—Juvenile literature. [1. Cities and towns.]
    I. Title. II. Series.
    HT119.N45 2002
    307.76—dc21   2001000965

Manufactured in the United States of America
1 2 3 4 5 6 – AM – 07 06 05 04 03 02